Seven Love Letters

Revelation 2 and 3 in the Language of Jesus

Leo De Siqueira

Unveiled Publishing
Calgary, Canada
Seven Love Letters: Revelation 2 and 3 in the Language of Jesus

ISBN-13: 978-1-9995060-4-9

Printed in the United States of America and Canada.

DEDICATION

To Craig and Stephanie Hill. Thank you for pulling me up and pushing me forward. For seeing in me what I often didn't see in myself. And thank you for our covenant friendship. I am so grateful for each of you.

CONTENTS

PREFACE

WHY THIS BOOK?

The harsh tone of the Greek text is inescapable. Most of our modern Bibles are translations based on the Greek New Testament. So when I began to read the New Testament from the Aramaic language, it was like re-reading the Bible for the first time. The text came alive in a different way, and the burning love of God toward us permeated through the text more than I had ever seen.

And it was during my work on a broader project of mine,[1] while translating chapters 2 and 3 of John's Revelation, that this dichotomy became ever more apparent. The Jesus that is so often portrayed as harsh and even violent (Rev 2:23) is seen in a completely different light in the original Aramaic language. I was so awe struck by what I came across that I felt compelled by our Lord and Saviour to share it.

It is with great joy and reverential awe of our Lord Jesus that I present to you the seven letters to the seven churches in the Book of Revelation from the language of Jesus. My hope is that as you meditate on these words, you would experience a cleansing from religiosity, "by the washing of water with the word" (Eph 5:26).

---

[1] This project is a three-part series on the Book of Revelation entitled "Revelation: Dawn of This Age."

SO WHAT'S THE DEAL WITH ARAMAIC?

> *"We all fell to the ground, and I heard a voice saying to me in Aramaic, 'Saul, Saul, why do you persecute me? It is hard for you to kick against the goads.'" Acts 26:14 (NIV)*

Mel Gibson got it right when he used Aramaic as the spoken language of his movie, *The Passion of the Christ.* Aramaic is an older sister language of Hebrew (a Semitic language of the Middle East), and is very close to it in its construction, alphabet, and vocabulary. Aramaic is related to Hebrew much like Portuguese is related to Spanish. It was the language of the surrounding Mesopotamian empires for centuries (Persia, Assyria, Babylon, etc.), much like the countries that surround Brazil speak Spanish, while in Brazil Portuguese is spoken.[2]

Aramaic is the language found in one of the oldest Bibles in the world, the *Peshitta.* So what does "Peshitta" mean? It is a Syriac word meaning "simple," "straight," or "common." So the Peshitta Bible is the ancient Aramaic Bible, using the simple or common language of Jesus' day.

"The Gospels were written originally in the language of the Jews, which was Aramaic, and later translated into Greek, the language of the Roman Empire. Jesus instructed the apostles to go first to Jerusalem, all Judea, Samaria, and then the uttermost part of the earth – Acts 1:8. History confirms that this was the order of missionary activity. The Jews were the first to hear, and many of them did believe (See Acts 6:7). The church at Jerusalem was the center and birthplace of Christianity (See Acts 8:1-4,31). What missionary takes no Bible and gives no Bible to the people to whom he or she ministers? The people need the written word to sustain the preaching of the word. Aramaic was the language of the people."[3]

Consider the following passages from one of the most common translations to date, the New International Version (NIV):

---

[2] It is worth noting that the Jews stopped speaking Hebrew during their Babylonian captivity in the 6th century BC. This is part of the reason why the Book of Daniel was written in Aramaic.

[3] Rev. David Bauscher. "Divine Contact: Discovery of the Original New Testament." Apple Books, pp. 43-44

*"Some time later, Jesus went up to Jerusalem for one of the Jewish festivals. Now there is in Jerusalem near the Sheep Gate a pool, which in **Aramaic** is called Bethesda and which is surrounded by five covered colonnades." John 5:1-2 (NIV)*

*"When Pilate heard this, he brought Jesus out and sat down on the judge's seat at a place known as the Stone Pavement (which in **Aramaic** is Gabbatha)." John 19:13 (NIV)*

*"Carrying his own cross, he went out to the place of the Skull (which in Aramaic is called Golgotha). Many of the Jews read this sign, for the place where Jesus was crucified was near the city, and the sign was written in **Aramaic**, Latin and Greek." John 19:17,20 (NIV)*

*"When they heard him [Paul] speak to them in **Aramaic**, they became very quiet." Acts 22:2 (NIV)*

*"We all fell to the ground, and I heard a voice saying to me in **Aramaic**, 'Saul, Saul, why do you persecute me? It is hard for you to kick against the goads.'" Acts 26:14 (NIV)*

For those still hesitant toward the notion that the Aramaic preceded the Greek, here are some further points for consideration:

- The Assyrian, Babylonian and Medo-Persian Empires (the nations surrounding Israel) all spoke Aramaic. When the Ten Tribes of Israel were assimilated by the Assyrians, the Aramaic language would have become their norm over time. And when Daniel was captive under the Babylonians, he spoke Aramaic and his book was written in Aramaic too.
- Evidence suggests that from a cultural perspective, the Greek language was seen with disdain. Consider the following quote from the Babylonian Talmud:
  "At that time it was declared… cursed be he who taught his sons Greek."[4]
  Or, consider the Talmud in Soferim 1:7–8, speaking of when the Torah was translated into Greek, "[It] was as difficult [a time] for

[4] Babylonian Talmud, Tract Baba Kamma (The First Gate), Chapter 7, online: <https://www.sefaria.org/Bava_Kamma>.

the Jewish people as the day when the Golden Calf was made."

- Judeans were strongly opposed to Hellenization. This is perhaps best illustrated through the Maccabean Revolt.[5]
- The Septuagint (Greek translation of the first five books of the Old Testament) was created at the request of the Egyptian King Ptolemy II Philadelphus for the great library in Alexandria. It was not written for Judean use.[6]
- Josephus, a Jewish POW turned Roman historian, lamented in the introductory remarks of his great work, "Antiquities of the Jews," that it was painful for him to translate his great work from Aramaic into the Greek language.[7] He even went on to say,

  "For those of my own nation freely acknowledge that I far exceed them in the learning belonging to Jews: I have also taken a great deal of pains to obtain the learning of the Greeks, and understand the elements of the Greek language, although I have so long accustomed myself to speak our own tongue, that I cannot pronounce Greek with sufficient exactness… for our nation does not encourage those who learn the languages of many nations."[8]

  Consider the fact that the apostles were "unschooled" and "common men" (Acts 4:13). How then could they have written so eloquently in Greek, since an educated man like Josephus had struggled with the language?

- In Josephus' most famous historical work, *The Wars of the Jews*, he wrote these words:

  "I have proposed to myself, for the sake of such as live under the government of the Romans, to translate those books into the Greek tongue, which I formerly composed

---

[5] This event is celebrated even to this day through Hanukkah. And it was also commemorated during Jesus' day. Back then it was known as "Dedication Day" (See John 10:22).

[6] Josephus, *Antiquities of the Jews,* 1:10; 12:12–40, online: <www.penelope.uchicago.edu/josephus>.

[7] Ibid, 1:3–12. See also, Josephus, *Against Apion*, 1:3, 50.

[8] Ibid, 20:26.

> in the language of our country, and sent to the Upper Barbarians; Joseph, the son of Matthias, by birth a Hebrew, a priest also, and one who at first fought against the Romans myself, and was forced to be present at what was done afterwards."[9]

- The Roman Empire had two official languages: Latin and Greek. Latin was more formal, and state documents were most often written in Latin.
- Several works from Qumran, such as Enoch and Tobit, are preserved in both Aramaic and Hebrew versions.[10]
- Discrimination was evident even in the first days of the Church against Greeks. *"And in those days, when the number of the disciples was multiplied, there arose a murmuring of the Grecians [Jews] against the Hebrews, because their widows were neglected in the daily ministration."* Acts 6:1 (NKJV)
- An interesting reference is made in Acts 1:19 to the Aramaic language: "And it was known unto all the dwellers at Jerusalem; insomuch as that field is called in their proper tongue, Aceldama, that is to say, The field of blood." As Ewan MacLeod points out,

> "This phrase is made up from the Aramaic hakel meaning field, and dama meaning the blood. (The KJV is translated from Greek, and Greek has no letter h, and so hakel becomes acel or akel when written in Greek). But, critically, Aceldama cannot be Hebrew. It can only be Aramaic. In Hebrew, the word for field is not hakel – it is sadeh. In Hebrew, the equivalent phrase would be sadeh haDam. Aceldama uniquely and precisely identifies "our own tongue," the phrase used by both Josephus and the New Testament, as Aramaic, rather

---

[9] Josephus, *Wars of the Jews,* Preface 1:1, online: <www.penelope.uchicago.edu/josephus>.

[10] "Aramaic was the Near East 'lingua franca' of the Biblical period, and it is still used among several Christian communities today. Just like the Hebrew Scrolls, the majority of Aramaic manuscripts were written in standard 'square' (Jewish) script. Represented in the Dead Sea Scrolls are a variety of Aramaic dialects: Official Aramaic, Jewish Palestinian Aramaic, Nabatean, and Christian Palestinian Aramaic." The Leon Levy Dead Sea Scrolls Digital Library, 2019, online: <www.deadseascrolls.org.il/learn-about-the-scrolls/languages-and-scripts>

than Hebrew."[11]

- Matthew 5:22, 27:46, Mark 5:41, 7:34, John 20:16 and 1 Corinthians 16:22 are some examples of Aramaic, not Hebrew, words being quoted.
- In addition to Irenaeus, who I quoted above, Papias and Eusebius agreed that Matthew was not written in Greek, but in his native tongue.

Papias (c. 60–163), an early church father, disciple of John the Apostle and contemporary of Polycarp, wrote:

> "'So then Matthew wrote the oracles in the Hebrew language, and every one interpreted them as he was able.' And the same writer uses testimonies from the first Epistle of John and from that of Peter likewise. And he relates another story of a woman, who was accused of many sins before the Lord, which is contained in the Gospel according to the Hebrews. These things we have thought it necessary to observe in addition to what has been already stated."[12]

Eusebius, a fourth-century church father and historian, made several references to the Aramaic dialect of the apostles and their writings. Below are some of those references:

- "For Matthew, who had at first preached to the Hebrews, when he was about to go to other peoples, committed his Gospel to writing in his native tongue, and thus compensated those whom he was obliged to leave for the loss of his presence." (Eusebius, *Ecclesiastical History*, Book III, 24:6)

- "And in how many provinces Peter preached Christ and taught the doctrine of the new covenant to those of the circumcision is clear from his own words in his epistle already mentioned as undisputed, in which he writes to the Hebrews of the dispersion in Pontus, Galatia, Cappadocia, Asia, and Bithynia." (Eusebius, *Ecclesiastical History*, Book III, 4:2)

---

[11] Ewan MacLeod, *Discover Aramaic* (JesusSpokeAramaic.com, 2016) at 139, e-book.
[12] Eusebius, *Ecclesiastical History,* Book III, 39:16, online: <www.earlychristianwritings.com/eusebius.html>

- "For as Paul had written to the Hebrews in his native tongue, some say that the evangelist Luke, others that this Clement himself, translated the epistle." (Eusebius, *Ecclesiastical History*, Book III, 38:2)

- "The whole church [of Jerusalem] consisted then of believing Hebrews who continued from the days of the apostles until the siege which took place at this time; in which siege the Jews, having again rebelled against the Romans, were conquered after severe battles." (Eusebius, *Ecclesiastical History*, Book III, 5:2)

- "And he (Hegesippus) wrote of many other matters, which we have in part already mentioned, introducing the accounts in their appropriate places. And from the Syriac Gospel according to the Hebrews he quotes some passages in the Hebrew tongue, showing that he was a convert from the Hebrews, and he mentions other matters as taken from the unwritten tradition of the Jews." (Eusebius, *Ecclesiastical History*, Book IV, 22:7)

- Since, in the beginning of this work, we promised to give, when needful, the words of the ancient presbyters and writers of the Church, in which they have declared those traditions which came down to them concerning the canonical books, and since Irenæus was one of them, we will now give his words and, first, what he says of the sacred Gospels: 'Matthew published his Gospel among the Hebrews in their own language, while Peter and Paul were preaching and founding the church in Rome. After their departure Mark, the disciple and interpreter of Peter, also transmitted to us in writing those things which Peter had preached; and Luke, the attendant of Paul, recorded in a book the Gospel which Paul had declared.'" (Eusebius, *Ecclesiastical History*, Book V, 8:1-3)

- "Pantænus was one of these [Saints], and is said to have gone to India. It is reported that among persons there who knew of Christ, he found the Gospel according to Matthew, which had anticipated his own arrival. For Bartholomew, one of the apostles, had preached to them, and left with them the writing of Matthew in the Hebrew language, which they had preserved till that time." (Eusebius, *Ecclesiastical History*, Book V, 10:3)

- "He (Clement of Alexandria) says that the Epistle to the Hebrews is the work of Paul, and that it was written to the Hebrews in the

Hebrew language; but that Luke translated it carefully and published it for the Greeks, and hence the same style of expression is found in this epistle and in the Acts." (Eusebius, *Ecclesiastical History*, Book V, 14:2)

- "Among the four Gospels, which are the only indisputable ones in the Church of God under heaven, I (Origen) have learned by tradition that the first was written by Matthew, who was once a publican, but afterwards an apostle of Jesus Christ, and it was prepared for the converts from Judaism, and published in the Hebrew language." (Eusebius, *Ecclesiastical History*, Book VI, 25:4)

Lastly, several Biblical scholars have explained in great detail the Semitic (Aramaic and Hebrew) grammar that is imbedded in the Greek New Testament. Here are some to consider for further research on this topic:

- *An Aramaic Approach to the Gospels and Acts*, by Matthew Black
- *Documents of the Primitive Church*, and, *Our Translated Gospels*, by Charles Cutler Torrey
- *Semitisms of the Book of Acts*, by Max Wilcox
- *The Aramaic Origin of the Fourth Gospel*, by Charles Fox Burney
- *The Aramaic Origin of the Four Gospels*, by Frank Zimmerman

TRANSLATIONS FROM THE ARAMAIC

For the texts of Revelation itself, I provide my own translation from the language of Jesus: Aramaic. To satiate the curiosity of the scholarly, I have used as a base the BFBS and UBS Peshitta[13], along with the Syriac and Hebrew Peshitta NT based on George A. Kiraz's SEDRA 3 database, and cross references with the Crawford Codex. The Khabouris Peshitta text does not have the book of Revelation in it.

[13] The British and Foreign Bible Society B.F.B.S. and United Bible Society U.B.S. Text of the 1905/1920 Aramaic New Testament is said to be a Critical Text of about 42 Aramaic Manuscripts.

PROLOGUE: REVELATION CHAPTER 1

"The Revelation which came to John The Evangelist from God in Patmos, the island to which he was exiled by Nero Caesar."

The Syriac heading of chapter 1 of Revelation, found in the Crawford Manuscript (12th century AD).

John's Revelation; the Hisgalus (Hebrew), the Apocalypse (Greek), both mean the same thing in their respective native language: "to unveil". However, the true impact of these opening words of John's letter to his congregations in Asia Minor (modern day Turkey) and his brethren in Jerusalem was not so much that he was revealing mysteries and secrets (not to say he didn't), but rather, that his opening lines were a proclamation of what was accomplished on the Cross at Calvary and that the end of the transition of covenant eras had come. Having written, "The revelation [unveiling] of Jesus the Messiah," meant that Jesus was being revealed as the One who was about to take away the veil of the Old Covenant.

Picking up from Matthew 27:51, let's read how Paul uses the notion of 'the veil' when speaking of the Mosaic Covenant:

"Therefore, having such a hope, we use great boldness in our speech, and we are not like Moses, who used to put a veil over his face so that the sons

of Israel would not stare at the end of what was fading away. But their minds were hardened; for until this very day at the reading of the old covenant the same veil remains unlifted, because it is removed in Christ. But to this day whenever Moses is read, a veil lies over their hearts; but whenever someone turns to the Lord, the veil is taken away. Now the Lord is the Spirit, and where the Spirit of the Lord is, there is freedom. 2 Cor 3:12-17 (NASB)

The Messiah removes the veil. In this passage, Paul uses a double meaning for veil: first, that the Old Covenant blinds like a veil, and second, that the Old Covenant *is* a veil, one that only Jesus the Messiah can remove from the people of Israel. Now this point is key: only to those circumcised under the Law of Moses is there a veil, meaning if you're a Gentile like me, this doesn't apply to you! But to the Jews and proselytes of John's day, the veil remained so long as the Temple system and the sacrificial offerings were still in operation.

And so John, as the trumpet blower sounding the alarm that the destruction of Jerusalem, the Temple and the sacrificial system was about to take place, opens his letter by saying, "The revelation [unveiling] of Jesus the Messiah," meaning that Jesus was unveiled as the One who was about to remove the veil of the Old Covenant!

א *(v 1–3) "The unveiling*[14] *of Yeshua the Messiah, which God gave unto Him, to symbolize*[15] *it to His royal subjects, what has been permitted to occur in haste;*

and He knew when to send it in the hand of his angel to His royal

---

14 "The root word here 'reveal,' 'wave,' is stated in the plural form. And then the suffix in Aramaic can mean 'our', or alternatively, in Aramaic (& Hebrew) it is used to express intense emotion (the likely reading here), with a prime example being 'Hosanna' from Matthew 21:15, or 'mighty' from Revelation 5:2. However, on the Crawford Codex there are no seyame markings over this word to indicate the scribe read it as a plural noun. Even still, the grammar in the verse strongly indicate the reading is plural." Glaser, Greg. Glaser Translation Notes (Copperopolis: Logical Hierarchy, 2015), at 1.

15 "'He symbolized' – *Shooda* in Aramaic is an important key for unlocking the meaning of Revelation. Symbolic language and imagery is used throughout to represent eternal realities and future events, very similar to the prophesies of Daniel and Ezekiel and the visions Joseph had interpreted in Genesis." Baucher, David. The Aramaic Interlinear Peshitta Holy Bible, pp. 182.

> *subject John, who bore witness to the word of God and to the testimony of Jesus the Messiah – everything that he saw.*
>
> *Blessedness to the one who reads aloud and to the one who hears the words of this prophecy, and attentively watches for the things which are written in it; for the epoch season is at hand." (Aramaic)*

The destruction of Israel, Jerusalem and the Temple will take place very quickly ("hastily"). Verse 2 reads as if it was meant for public oration: "Blessed is he (singular) who reads, and those (plural) who hear." Lastly, we read that the "specific time" (zbn in Aramaic), meaning an "instance" or "season" was immediately upon them.

> א *(v 4–5) "John, to the seven messianic communities*[16] *in the province of Asia:*
>
> *Grace unto you, and shalom, from the One who is, who was, and who is coming, and from the sevenfold Spirit before his throne, and from Yeshua the Messiah;*
>
> *the faithful witness, the firstborn from the dead, preeminent over the rulers of the earth. Him who burns with love for us, and unfettered us from our sins through His blood." (Aramaic)*

The early church was founded and mostly comprised of Messianic Jews; Jewish people who had embraced Jesus as their Messiah. John's letter was clearly written to a Jewish audience, as I will point out often.

---

16 'Idoto', is one word, literally meaning "an assembly of witnesses." In Greek, ecclesia, what we call "church" today. I have chosen to add context into the translation: these were assemblies or communities of believers who bore witness, or testified, to the fact that Jesus was the Messiah. They were communities *of* the Messiah, hence, messianic communities. That said, I am by no means advocating for or against Messianic Judaism. Therefore the reader should note that the translation employed is unrelated to any sort of modern movements.

THE JEWISHNESS OF THE EARLY CHURCH

> *"You worship what you do not know; we worship what we know, for salvation is from the Jews." John 4:22 (NASB)*

It is important that I preface this section by clarifying my intention. There is no subversive plot to lead the reader to conclude that there is any sort of dualism or tiered status between Jew and Gentile. Nor is it my intention to lead the reader to conclude that they must adhere to the Law of Moses and embrace a legalistic lifestyle. Far from it. Rather, my approach here is a historical one. It is imperative that we have an accurate social-historical awareness of the text if we ever have a hope of properly understanding it.

In other words, while the Bible is timeless, it was also written over a period of several hundred years, by different people in different circumstances. Revelation is no different. Our Western culture has become obsessed with taking this book and repackaging it to fit our Western culture and theology. To separate John's Apocalypse from its Jewish roots is to take the Epistle to the Hebrews and say it was written for Gentiles. Therefore, my effort here is to restore Revelation to its proper context in order to set a proper foundation from which we can launch our exegesis. Let us now move into the topic at hand.

> The Jewish Christians instinctively regarded their new faith as but a further expression of their national religion; the Temple continued to be the central shrine at which they worshipped and many of their members became distinguished for their zealous observance of the Law. To such men the tradition of Israel's unique status with God was a matter of fervent belief, and we have seen something of the grudging and qualified consent which they gave to the admittance of certain favoured Gentiles to participation in the privileges of their new faith."[17]

---

[17] S. G. F. Brandon, M.A., D.D., *The Fall of Jerusalem and the Christian Church,*

It wasn't until after Jesus ascended that His own followers finally got the memo: that God's Grand Love Story, the Eternal Gospel, was not exclusively for the descendants of Abraham (see Acts 10:9-16). But how could this be? Perhaps because they failed to pivot from the initial mission:

> *"These twelve Jesus sent out after instructing them: "Do not go in the way of the Gentiles, and do not enter any city of the Samaritans; but rather go to the lost sheep of the house of Israel." Matt 10:5–6 (NASB)*

But we do see a gradual shift from Israel-only to Judea, Samaria and the ends of the earth, albeit long after the Great Commission and Ascension (Matt 28:18–20 in light of Acts 10:9-16). Nevertheless, the first-followers of Yeshua were predominately Jewish. In fact, although Paul was the "Apostle to the Gentiles," preaching abroad in the Roman Empire, his primary strategy was to go into cities and towns that had a Jewish presence, and preach first in their local Synagogues.[18]

Below are some Scriptures that remind us of the fact that the early church was not a Gentile majority led by a handful of Jewish Apostles. It was in fact a Jewish majority led by Jewish Apostles. While it seems this phenomenon did not last long past the fall of Jerusalem in 70 AD, it is still an important factor that anchors our interpretation.

> *"…Those who were scattered because of the persecution that occurred in connection with Stephen made their way to Phoenicia and Cyprus and Antioch, speaking the word to no one except to Jews alone. But there were some of them, men of Cyprus and Cyrene, who came to Antioch and began speaking to the Greeks also… [And] news about them reached the ears of the church at Jerusalem." Acts 11:19–22 (NASB)*

> *"After we [Paul and Luke] arrived in Jerusalem, the brethren received us gladly… And when they heard it they began glorifying God; and they said to him, "You see, brother, how many thousands there are among the Jews of those who have believed, and they are all zealous for the Law; and they have been told about you, that you are teaching all the Jews* ***who are among the Gentiles****…" Acts 21:17, 20, 21 (NASB)*

A Study of the Effects of the Jewish Overthrow of A.D. 70 on Christianity (London: S.P.C.K, 1951) at 71.

[18] See, Viola, Frank. The Untold Story of the New Testament Church: An Extraordinary Guide to Understanding the New Testament (p. 74). Destiny Image. Kindle Edition.

"Therefore remember that previously you, the Gentiles… were at that time separate from Christ, excluded from the people of Israel, and strangers to the covenants of the promise, having no hope and without God in the world. But now in Christ Jesus you who previously were far away have been brought near by the blood of Christ…

"For this reason I, Paul, [am] the prisoner of Christ Jesus for the sake of you Gentiles… by revelation there was made known to me the mystery, as I wrote before briefly… which in other generations was not made known to mankind, as it has now been revealed to His holy apostles and prophets in the Spirit; to be specific, that the Gentiles are fellow heirs and fellow members of the body, and fellow partakers of the promise in Christ Jesus through the gospel." Eph 2:11–13, 3:1, 3, 5–6 (NASB)

"Now if [the Jewish] transgression is riches for the world and their failure is riches for the Gentiles, how much more will their fulfillment be! But I am speaking to you who are Gentiles…

"But if some of the branches were broken off, and you, being a wild olive, were grafted in among them and became partaker with them of the rich root of the olive tree, do not be arrogant toward the branches; but if you are arrogant, remember that it is not you who supports the root, but the root supports you. You will say then, "Branches were broken off so that I might be grafted in." Quite right, they were broken off for their unbelief, but you stand by your faith. Do not be conceited, but fear; for if God did not spare the natural branches, He will not spare you, either…

"For I do not want you, brethren, to be uninformed of this mystery—so that you will not be wise in your own estimation—that a partial hardening has happened to Israel until the fullness of the Gentiles has come in; 26 and so all Israel will be saved…"
Rom 11:12, 13, 17–21, 25–26 (NASB)

"On this account be remembering that at one time, you, the Gentiles in the flesh, the ones habitually called uncircumcision by that which is called circumcision in the flesh made by hand, that you were at that time without a Messiah, alienated from the commonwealth of the Israel and strangers from the covenants of the promise, not having hope and without God in the world.

"Therefore remember that previously you, the Gentiles… remember that you were at that time separate from Christ, excluded from the people of Israel, and strangers to the covenants of the promise, having no hope and without God in the world. But now in Christ Jesus you who previously were far away have been brought near by the blood of Christ…
And He came and preached peace to you who were far away… So then you are no longer strangers and foreigners, but you are fellow citizens with the saints, and are of God's household, having been built on the foundation of the apostles and prophets, Christ Jesus Himself being the cornerstone."
Eph 2:11–13, 17–20 (NASB)

Despite all that we have just read, it was still to my surprise that I discovered that Revelation was written to a Jewish audience concerning life-altering Jewish issues: the end of the Mosaic Age, the destruction of the Holy Temple, the end of the sacrificial system, and the extinction of the Temple priesthood. All of these things took place historically in 70 AD. Revelation seeks, therefore, to help the Jews make sense of *why* these things happened from a theological perspective.[19] I did not think this way going into the text. Rather, the analysis of the Aramaic text itself presented these findings. I would liken the experience to the romanticized notions we have of archeological adventure and discovery seen in the *Indiana Jones* movies!

REVELATION 1:6–7

- א *(v 6): "And He has made us the priestly kingdom to His God and Father—to Him be glory and dominion to the age of ages. Amen."*

The priestly kingdom echoes the Torah: "'and you shall be to Me a kingdom of priests and a holy nation.' These are the words that you shall speak to the sons of Israel" (Exodus 19:6). Peter also reminds us of this truth: "But you are a chosen race, a royal priesthood, a holy nation, a people for God's own possession, so that you may proclaim the excellencies of Him who has called you out of darkness into His marvelous light" (1 Peter 2:9).

- א *(v 7): "Behold! He comes with clouds, and every eye will see Him, but especially those who pierced Him, and all the generations of the Land will mourn over Him. Yes and amen."*

---

[19] This theme is discussed at length in my book, Revelation: Dawn of This Age.

Jesus spoke words similar to these in John's presence approximately 37 years earlier, saying,

"Upon you will fall the guilt of all the righteous blood shed on earth… Truly I say to you, all these things will come upon this generation.

Jerusalem, Jerusalem, who kills the prophets and stones those who are sent to her! How often I wanted to gather your children together, the way a hen gathers her chicks under her wings, and you were unwilling. Behold, your house is being left to you desolate! For I say to you, from now on you will not see Me until you say, 'Blessed is He who comes in the name of the Lord!'" Matt 23:37–39 (NASB)

Revelation 1:7 is charged with prophetic language, echoing Daniel 7:13 and Zechariah 12:10–14. Both prophets, and specifically the chapters quoted, spoke to the transition of epoch seasons that took place during the 40-year period from 30 to 70 AD. Now, Jesus comes to John to say that the transition period was about to reach it's climactic ending.

The coming of the Lord Jesus to bring about an end to the Mosaic Age in 70 AD is the only context in which the final interaction between Jesus and his disciples in John 21 makes sense.

> *"Peter turned around and saw the disciple whom Jesus loved following them—the one who also had leaned back on His chest at the supper and said, 'Lord, who is the one who is betraying You?' So Peter, upon seeing him, said to Jesus, 'Lord, and what about this man?' Jesus said to him, "'f I want him to remain until I come, what is that to you? You follow Me!' Therefore this account went out among the brothers, that that disciple [John] would not die; yet Jesus did not say to him that he would not die, but only, 'If I want him to remain until I come, what is that to you?' John 21:20–23 (NASB)*

John was literally the only one who remained until Jesus came. By the time the Mosaic Age came to an end via the destruction of the Temple, all the other disciples has been killed, save for John. And to be clear, Jesus didn't cause the destruction, but rather, He brought about the time for contractual obligations of the Law to be requisite. **Jesus' return signaled the day of fulfilment of Moses' prophecies in Deuteronomy 28:15–68, 29:22–30:10, 31:14–22, and 32:1–43.**[20]

---

[20] Please take time to read through them, as they will greatly increase one's understanding of why the fall of Jerusalem in 70 AD took place.

This was after a 40 year period of grace, where through the disciples of Jesus, God pleaded with Israel to turn from their sins (from 30 to 70 AD), just as He had done in the days of Moses. During those 40 years, an entire generation died in the wilderness, and a new generation crossed over the River Jordan under Joshua (Yehoshua, a type of Yeshua, Jesus).

Now where it says, "all the tribes of the Land," most translations will read, "all the tribes of the earth." But this is misleading. One major error with most translations is the rendering of the word "land" as "earth". The Complete Jewish Bible accurately translates verse 7: "all the tribes of the Land will mourn him." From a literary perspective, both the Greek and Aramaic here agreed that "land" is the proper word choice, not "earth" or "planet." This was an isolated incident. And I've already made a case for "The Land" meaning "The Land of Israel" in book one, so I won't digress here. Suffice to say, whenever you read "The Land," to the Jewish reader then and even today (see the modern Israeli newspaper, *Haaretz*; literally, "The Land"!) it was a given that it was in reference to the Land of Israel.

From a contextual perspective, because verse 7 is alluding to Zechariah 12, we know for certain that it speaks to the Holy Land exclusively because Zechariah 12–14 has to do with Jerusalem. Those chapters of Zechariah are hard to interpret. But I believe they span the entirety of the Messianic Age we are currently in. Several times between chapters 12 to 14 we have references to the destruction of Jerusalem and the transition period from the Mosaic to Messianic Era. And at other points in chapters 12 to 14 of Zechariah we see what God will do at the end of the Messianic Era, coinciding with what John saw in Revelation 20:8–10.

THE ALPHA AND OMEGA – THE ALEPH AND TAV

> א *(v 8) "I am the Aleph and the Tav," says the Lord Elohim, "who is and who was and who is coming, the Almighty."*

It is interesting to note that the earliest manuscripts lack, "the Beginning and the End" here. It is possibly an addition from later copies in order to have fluidity, since Revelation 22:13 does have, "the Beginning and the End" in early manuscripts. So sticking with the Aramaic, verse 8 reads, "I am the Aleph and the Tav," which in Greek translates as Alpha and Omega.

We know John's native tongue was Aramaic. This was the language he spoke growing up, and the language he would have conversed with Jesus during the Messiah's earthly ministry. Therefore I will venture to suggest that John would have heard words of his encounter with Jesus and the angels in Aramaic, even if he only internalized them as thought. If you are bilingual like myself, you can appreciate the reality that you will often think in your native tongue. Whatever language(s) you learn after your native tongue, you are still likely to think and have self-talk in your native tongue, depending on how much you use it. So even though John may have written his letter to a Greek speaking audience, I would like to propose that he received and interpreted the information in his native tongue. This is a concept that I will also revisit at key points throughout this writing.

Why does this matter? Because things get really cool when we get into ancient Hebrew! The words Alpha and Omega are Greek. But if John were to have heard them in Hebrew, Jesus would have said, "I am the Aleph and the Tav." And this is where things get interesting.

Ancient Hebrew pictography for Aleph is representative of God Himself. The roots of this are based on the image of an ox, representing power, strength and authority. The letters that make up the word Aleph enhance the imagery. The ל represents both a shepherds staff and a sceptre of authority. Combined with the א (ox) it was seen as a yoke of an ox. This is where we get deeper meaning of Jesus' words in Matthew 11:29-30,

> *"Take My yoke upon you and learn from Me, for I am gentle and lowly in heart, and you will find rest for your souls. For My yoke is easy and My burden is light."*

It was customary for the elder oxen to be yoked to a younger one in order that the apprenticing bull may learn from the experienced one. I find this to be mind blowing in the context of being yoked with Christ.

The last letter, ף, is often omitted from pictography since Aleph is just based on the root אל. Nevertheless, ף is part of the final word and so in my opinion has significance. Pey (ף) represents the mouth and the power of the spoken word. This is why John wrote a few verses later that he saw proceeding from the mouth of Jesus, "a sharp two-edged sword" (1:16).

So Jesus is the Alpha, or the Aleph in Hebrew, which still means that he is the beginning in the sense that He is the Creator and the I AM. But in addition to this, etymologically He is the God of all authority, the shepherd who has yoked Himself to us in order to guide and teach, who by the word of his mouth speaks forth and His will is accomplished. How amazing is that!

We also know that He is the Omega, which in Hebrew is the Tav. Tav in ancient Hebrew has a broad depth of meaning that is multi-layered. First, it's most basic meaning is that it is a sign or a mark (see Ezek 9:4 and Job 31:35 in a translation that supports earlier manuscripts). The significance that is derived from Ezekiel is that the mark represented Passover, or salvation. For a mark was placed over the door posts of the Hebrews that told the angel to "pass over" their house.

And the meaning we derive in Job for the word Tav is that it is a binding agreement of a legal document, such as a covenant. Furthermore, the inscription of the letter itself when in early Hebrew was simply an upright cross, or our modern day "t". It is quite likely that the mark that Ezekiel was instructed to mark upon foreheads in chapter 9 of his book was in fact the sign of the cross! And in Jewish mystic tradition, the Tav is associated with truth, law, seals of authority, simple faith and even the power of resurrection.

So Jesus is also the Omega, or the Tav, which means he is the ender, as in the author and finisher of our faith (Heb 12:2), the One who rules in and outside of time. Additionally, He is also the One who signed with his seal our New Covenant of salvation, a binding marriage agreement. And this legal document was inscribed with the mark of the cross upon which he was crucified. One could summarize as follows: As the Aleph and the Tav, Jesus is the supreme and eternal ruling shepherd and the God who forged an eternal covenant which He signed with His seal. That is worth a selah.

One final note on Aleph. This also plants a seed for a later discussion when we visit chapter 20 of Revelation. In addition to Aleph being the first letter of the Hebrew alphabet and its meaning being a supreme leader and a yoke of discipleship, it also has one other definition: the consonants of the word can also mean the number 1000 (see Strong's: #0441 and #0505).

First, Aleph can mean a military commander of a thousand troops. The same is also true for the Greek. Chilioi (χίλιοι, "1000") is expanded to chilliarch, "captain of 1000". And using the same root consonants, אלף (read, 'eleph) is the numerical value of 1000. If you look at Revelation 20, this notion even connects to the 1000 year reign of Christ.

א *(v 9) "I, John, your brother and forthwith your companion in the affliction and in the perseverance which are in Jesus,*
was on the island called Patmos because of the testimony of Yeshua the Messiah."

The word most translations have in place of "affliction" here is "tribulation," and this word is the source of much debate and confusion in our present Western culture. But it merely means calamity or affliction. The same word is found in 1 Thessalonians 1:6 and James 5:13. The "pre-trib" vs "post-trib" jargon that has prevailed in the 20th century is completely foreign to the text and proper eschatology in general. **The questions every reader must ask are: what was afflicting the first-century Jewish church, and, what were they persevering towards?**

> "There is now the reference to persecution in the First Thessalonian Epistle to be considered. In this Paul draws a parallel between the sufferings of his converts at the hands of their compatriots and those of the members of the Judaean churches at the hands of the Jews. This statement and its immediate sequel, in which, after making some condemnatory observations about the persecuting activity of the Jews, he includes himself, or his party, among the objects of this persecution, would clearly constitute evidence for believing that the Jewish Christians in Palestine notably suffered for their faith at the hands of their country- men."[21]

John was on the receiving end of the same affliction as his flock. And John and his Jewish brethren were patiently waiting for something to take place in *their* lifetime. This affliction was the same thorn Paul spoke of that was in his flesh: persecution from the "Judaizers." Those who sought to undermine the apostolic work taking place in the Holy Land and the Empire.

Consider the following Scriptures:

- *"Do not go in the way of the Gentiles, and do not enter any city of the Samaritans; but rather go to the lost sheep of the house of Israel…*

  Behold, I [Jesus] send you out as sheep in the midst of wolves; so be shrewd as serpents and innocent as doves. But beware of men, for they will hand you over to the courts and scourge you in their synagogues; and you will even be brought before governors and

[21] S. G. F. Brandon, M.A., D.D., *The Fall of Jerusalem and the Christian Church, A Study of the Effects of the Jewish Overthrow of A.D. 70 on Christianity* (London: S.P.C.K, 1951) at 92.

kings for My sake, as a testimony to them and to the Gentiles…

"Brother will betray brother to death, and a father his child; and children will rise up against parents and cause them to be put to death. You will be hated by all because of My name, but it is the one who has endured to the end who will be saved.

"But whenever they persecute you in one city, flee to the next; for truly I say to you, you will not finish going through the cities of Israel until the Son of Man comes."
Matt 10:5–6, 16–18, 21–23 (NASB)

- *"For nation will rise against nation, and kingdom against kingdom, and in various places there will be famines and earthquakes. But all these things are merely the beginning of birth pangs.*

  "Then they will deliver you to tribulation, and will kill you, and you will be hated by all nations because of My name…

  But the one who endures to the end, he will be saved. This gospel of the kingdom shall be preached in the whole [known] world as a testimony to all the nations, and then the end will come.

  "Therefore when you see the abomination of desolation which was spoken of through Daniel the prophet, standing in the holy place (let the reader understand), then those who are in Judea must flee to the mountains." Matt 24:7–9, 13–16 (NASB)

- *"A great persecution began against the church in Jerusalem, and they were all scattered throughout the regions of Judea and Samaria, except the apostles." Acts 8:1 (NASB)*

Twice in Matthew Jesus connects the preaching of the Gospel to the Jews in Judea and the Jews spread abroad (the Diaspora, the "Ten Lost Tribes") to the end of the Mosaic Age, culminating in the destruction of the Temple (hence, "flee to the mountains" to escape the Roman invasion in 70 AD). The Messianic followers of Jesus were patiently enduring the hardship He had warned them about. If they could persevere until the end of this transition period, they would be delivered.

As for John being on Patmos, we don't know for sure why he was there. It could have been banishment, but that doesn't imply imprisonment. Or it may be that he was preaching the Gospel there and trying to establish a new community of believers.

> א *(v 10–11): "And I was in the Spirit on the first day of the week, and I heard from behind me a great voice, like a shofar, Who said, "That which you are seeing, write in a book and send to the seven messianic communities:*
>
> *To Ephesus, and to Smyrna, and to Pergamum, and to Thyatira, and to Sardis, and to Philadelphia, and to Laodicea."*

Why did Jesus pick these churches out of all the ones He could have chosen from? Perhaps we will never know fully, but here are some of my thoughts as to the intentionality of Jesus in addressing these communities of Jewish followers:

1. John's flock: John was not only an Apostle. He also held a prophetic office. The message came to him first. It would make sense then that his congregations would become co-labourers in the spreading of this message throughout the Diaspora (Jews spread abroad, outside the Holy Land), and perhaps even within Judea.

2. No apostles: If John did in fact receive this visitation from the Lord circa 66–67 AD, then there may have been few (if any) surviving Apostles (the original 11), as many of the others had been martyred. John was perhaps the only remaining original disciple with a large network of followers. Others were too remote, like Thomas for example, who was likely in India at the time. In fact, it was the Jews from this region that were ultimately responsible for Paul's Roman imprisonment (see Acts 21:27).

   > "Tradition holds that 11 of the Twelve Apostles were martyred. Peter, Andrew, and Philip were crucified; James the Greater and Thaddaeus fell to the sword; James the Lesser was beaten to death while praying for his attackers; Bartholomew was flayed alive and then crucified; Thomas and Matthew were speared; Matthias was stoned to death;

and Simon was either crucified or sawed in half. John—the last survivor of the Twelve—likely died peaceably, possibly in Ephesus…"[22]

3. Location: Anatolia (Western Asia Minor) was the gateway between the West (Rome) and the East (Israel). John and his followers were strategically located along a major trade route that began at the Hellespont (known today as the Dardanelles) and traversed longitudinally all the way through Antioch of Syria and beyond. Roman Jews on pilgrimage to Jerusalem for one of the feasts would have had to pass through the seven cities of Revelation. Another person who rode through this trade road was Vespasian enroute from Greece to Israel when Nero had dispatched him to destroy the Holy Land.

"The Jews also obtained honours from the Kings of Asia, when they became their auxiliaries. For Seleucus Nicator made them citizens in those cities which he built in Asia… and gave them privileges equal to those of the Macedonians and Greeks…

We also know, that Marcus Agrippa was of the like disposition towards the Jews. For when the people of Ionia were very angry at them, and besought Agrippa that they, and they only might have those privileges of citizens, which Antiochus, the grandson of Seleucus, who by the Greeks was called the God, had bestowed on them; and desired that if the Jews were to be joint-partakers with them, they might be obliged to worship the gods they themselves worshipped: but when these matters were brought to the trial, the Jews prevailed, and obtained leave to make use of their own customs."[23]

4. Spiritual Location: Anatolia was once the kingdom of Gyges of Lydia, with Sardis as it's capital. Gyges of Lydia is the Greek name for the same man who in Assyria was known as Gugu Ma-Gugu, which in Hebrew is rendered Gog of Ma-Gog. The historical king who became

[22] Andrew Todhunter, *In the Footsteps of the Apostles,* National Geographic Magazine, March 2012 Issue.
[23] Josephus, *Antiquities of the Jews,* By William Whiston, M.A. (London: University of Cambridge, 1737) at 3:1–2.

synonymous with Jewish lore of long-standing antagonists of God's people was used by Ezekiel and John to illustrate God's sovereign plan to stay the opponents of His people once and for all (much more on this subject in book three).

5. **The New Epicenter: Lastly and most importantly, the location of the central-hub of the Jesus movement would experience a radical shift in the first-century AD.** The Jerusalem Church was the undisputed headquarters of the Messianic Jews, with James, Peter and John as the resident leaders (Acts 15; Gal 2). After the fall of Jerusalem in 70 AD, Asia Minor grew in influence for 1000 years, until the Great East-West Schism of 1054 AD.

   The Roman Empire was not the first to adopt Christianity. It was the nations of Armenia in 301 and Georgia in 327, both situated in Asia Minor. The First Christian Council outside Jerusalem was held in Nicaea (of the Nicaean Creed fame), which is in Asia Minor, in 325 AD. Another Council was held in Constantinople in 381 (Asia Minor), followed by subsequent Councils in Ephesus in 431 (Asia Minor), and Chalcedon in 451 (Asia Minor).

> "The Church at Caesarea after A.D. 70 would probably have been the chief centre of Christianity in Palestine, being composed mainly of Gentiles, who would certainly have constituted the more influential party after the Jewish national disaster. As such the Caesarean Church is likely to have inherited certain traditions of the original Jerusalem Church and a considerable respect for its memory."[24]

Caesarea and Antioch were well known centres for followers of Jesus. But it was the churches of Ephesus and Smyrna that grew in renown[25] and thus tilted the centrality of our Faith from the Levant to Asia Minor after Jerusalem was destroyed. **And perhaps this is why John, the last surviving leader of the Jerusalem church, was sent to Asia Minor to tend to the**

---

[24] S. G. F. Brandon, M.A., D.D., *The Fall of Jerusalem and the Christian Church, A Study of the Effects of the Jewish Overthrow of A.D. 70 on Christianity* (London: S.P.C.K, 1951) at 43.
[25] See Ignatius' letters to the Ephesians and the Smyrnaeans.

work Paul began there.[26]

> "[After] A.D. 70 the Church of Jerusalem disappears completely from the life and concern of the Church... In the period before we see the Church strongly centralized around the mother community of Jerusalem, whose authority and prestige are unchallenged, even by the daring Paul. From this period, which is so well illumined b i the writings of Paul and the narrative of Acts, we pass on in our survey to find the life of the Church [in Jerusalem] disappearing into obscurity..."[27]

THE PRIESTLY DESCRIPTION OF JESUS

It is one thing to read Hebrews 8 and to know theologically that Jesus is our High Priest. But it is a whole other level to know this experientially! John *saw* Jesus adorned as the High Priest in a mesmerizing encounter with his beloved friend and Messiah.

> א *(v 12–17) And I turned to intimately know that voice who spoke with me, and when I turned around, I saw seven menorahs of gold;*
>
> *And in the midst of the menorahs as the likeness of a man, and he wore an ephod and he was girded around his chest with a golden sash.*
>
> *His head and his hair were white like wool and like snow, and his eyes were like flames of fire. And His feet were in the likeness of the brass of Lebanon*[28] *which is heated in a furnace, and his voice was*

---

[26] The soil upon which Jerusalem stood did not remain void. History tells us that a Roman city was built on top of Jerusalem's ruins, named Aelia Capitolina. It had a church community within it, and early church father Hegesippus was a part of it.
[27] S. G. F. Brandon, M.A., D.D., *The Fall of Jerusalem and the Christian Church, A Study of the Effects of the Jewish Overthrow of A.D. 70 on Christianity* (London: S.P.C.K, 1951) at 183.
[28] The Greek of Westcott & Hort's edition has 'Burnished brass' - neuter noun, dative case matched with 'Burning' - feminine noun, genitive case; this is a grammatical 'no, no' in Greek. Both case & gender should agree for these two words. The Greek seems also to be an invented word, not occurring elsewhere in Greek lit. It appears a translator made a compound Greek word out of two Aramaic words 'Brass' & 'Lebanon,' which did not exist before and confused all the

like the voice of many waters.

And there exists in his right hand seven stars, and a sharp sword[29] *proceeding from his mouth, and I saw Him*[30] *like the sun radiating in its intensity.*

There are five major references to the priestly garments of Aaron the Priest in Revelation chapters 1 to 3. Why this matters to us is because we must understand that the office of the High Priest was the most honored and esteemed of all for Jews. He was a big deal. He was the only one who would go into the Temple once a year and offer sacrifices for the atonement of Israel's sins. Jesus then became the ultimate, super-human, super-natural High Priest.

"Now the main point in what has been said is this: we have such a high priest, who has taken His seat at the right hand of the throne of the Majesty in the heavens, a minister in the sanctuary and in the true tabernacle, which the Lord set up, not man…
But now He [Jesus] has obtained a more excellent ministry, to the extent that He is also the mediator of a better covenant, which has been enacted on better promises…
When He said, 'A new covenant,' He has made the first obsolete. But whatever is becoming obsolete and growing old is about to disappear."
Heb 8:1–2, 6 (NASB)

Jesus was seen in the heavenly tabernacle, and Moses made a copy of what already existed in heaven (Heb 8:5–6). He stood beside the Menorah, the golden lampstand (Ex 25:31–40), and alluding to Aaron, the first High Priest, Jesus was seen in a sacerdotal ephod, the priestly garment.

"Aaron shall enter the Holy Place with this: with a bull as a sin offering and a ram as a burnt offering. He shall put on the holy linen tunic, and the linen undergarments shall be next to his body, and he shall be wrapped about the waist with the linen sash and the linen turban wound around his forehead (these are holy garments)." Lev 16:3–4 (NASB)

And in Exodus we read,

---

translators. Most translations of the Greek have, 'Burnished brass' as the meaning." Bauscher, Glenn David, The Aramaic English Interlinear Peshitta Bible, pp. 2744.

29 "Sword" can also be translated as "spear" or "lance." See Jennings', pp. 205.

30 "From the Aramaic Crawford reading, "and I saw Him."

> *"And you shall make holy garments for Aaron your brother, for glory and for beauty… make Aaron's garments to consecrate him, that he may serve as priest to Me. And these are the garments which they shall make: a breastplate, an ephod, a robe, a tunic of checkered work, a turban, and a sash." Ex 28:2–4 (NASB)*

If Aaron's ephod was made for glory and for beauty, how much more Jesus! And there will be more priestly garment descriptions in chapters 2 and 3 of Revelation. The vision of Jesus as high priest would have immediately resounded with the first century Jewish audience that Jesus came to. And as Hebrews 8:6 pointed out, the Messianic Covenant made the Mosaic Covenant obsolete, and now it was time for that covenant to disappear.

א *(v 17–18) "And when I saw him, I fell at his feet as one dead, and he laid his right hand upon me saying,*
'Fear not! I am the First and the Last; and am he who lives, but became dead, and behold! I am alive unto the age of ages, amen.
And I have the key of Death and of Sheol."

In the Aramaic Jesus states that He has authority to bind and loose, open and shut (hence "keys"; see Matt 16:17–19) Death and Sheol. This statement has profound theological implications. Especially since both Death and Sheol will be destroyed *prior* to heaven and earth being renewed.

א *(v 19) "Write henceforth what you have seen, and things that are and prepared to come to pass after these."*

This breakdown is significant to helping us understand the chronology of John's visions. The Aramaic agrees with the above translation, where the connective "and" links three timeframes: past, present and future. Here is a simple framework of Revelation's order of events:

- Past (what John beheld): 4, 5, 12,
- Present (what is): 1–3, 6–11, 13–20a, 22
- Future (after these things): 20b, 21

The key thing here is to remember that these timestamps are relative to when John was receiving the vision (say 67 AD), not when you are reading his vision 2000 years later!

א *(v 20) "The mystery of the seven stars which you saw upon my right hand and the seven menorahs: seven stars are the angels*[31] *of the seven messianic communities, and the seven menorahs of gold which you saw are the seven messianic communities."*

Every time you read lampstand in Revelation replace it in your head with a menorah. The Aramaic specifically uses the word menorah.[32] This again illustrates that Jesus was speaking primarily to a Jewish audience who would be receiving grave news concerning their homeland, their symbolic place of worship (Temple), and their kinsmen; the ~1,000,000 Jews slaughtered and 97,000 enslaved[33] by Vespasian and Titus in 70 AD. John's Revelation was as primary to the people of Israel as Paul's Corinthian letters were primary to the Gentiles in Corinth.

---

[31] In almost every other instance this word is used in the NT, it is translated as "angel." There is no reason to deviate here by translating the word as "messenger." The Hebrew and Aramaic are the same, in which the word angel and messenger are one. Context determines translation. For instance, Matt 11:10, John the Baptist is a messenger (same word here).

[32] Strong's G3087.

[33] According to Josephus, Jewish Wars, 6:9:3.

1 FIRST LOVE LETTER: EPHESUS

This is the famous church of Ephesus! They are the ones to whom Paul wrote, "[I have] heard of the faith in the Lord Jesus which exists among you and your love for all the saints." (Eph 1:15). This theme of love is one that Jesus will pick up on, as we will read below.

For context, you may liken Ephesus to Boston, Massachusetts. It was a major port city, a large center for trade, and boasted massive agoras (shopping malls). Ephesus even superseded Pergamum as the Roman capital of Asia Minor in the mid-first-century AD. It was also home to the goddess Artemis, the "goddess of love." Her temple was huge, and patrons came from all over to pay homage and to employ the services of the temple harlots in worship.

One textual note just before we begin. At the start of each letter you will read, "To *the messenger (or angel) of the congregation*," which is the literal Aramaic translation. Historically, we know this was a direct reference to the Jewish assemblies of their day. In the synagogues, "there was the *Sheliach Tsibbur* or 'messenger of the congregation,' who read the prayers."[34] This messenger could also be known as the "angel of the assembly".[35] Jesus was clearly addressing a predominately Jewish audience.

REVELATION 2:1–7

> "And to the messenger[36] who is in the messianic community[37] of Ephesus write: 'Thus says he who holds the seven stars in his hand, he who walks amongst the menorahs of gold:
>
> 'I know your works, and your toil, and your patience, and that you are not able to tolerate evil, and you have tested those who say to themselves that they are Apostles, and they are not, and you have found them false. And you have patience and you have endured because of my name and you have not grown weary.
>
> 'Except there is this that concerns me about you:[38] That first love of yours, you abandoned it. Cause yourself to remember

---

[34] The Ancient Synagogue Service, Ernest De Witt Burton, Vol. 8, No. 2 (Aug., 1896), pp. 143-148 Published by: The University of Chicago Press.

[35] See, Palestine: The Physical Georgraphy And Natural History Of The Holy Land By Kitto, John, London: Charles Knight & Co.. Very Good. 1841, pp. 806; Samuel Burder, Oriental Customs, Michigan: University of Michigan, 1923, pp. 387;

[36] Identical to the Hebrew, malak (Strong's H4397), messenger is the same word for angel. It carries a missional or occupational sense. Context determines if we use angel or messenger. Because Jesus is speaking to John, it wouldn't make sense for John to then relay these words to heaven's angels. Rather, the first century Jews are being commissioned to share with one another these exhortations.

[37] As noted earlier, 'Idoto', is one word, literally meaning "an assembly of witnesses." In Greek, ecclesia, what we call "church" today. I have chosen to add context into the translation: these were assemblies or communities of believers who bore witness, or testified, to the fact that Jesus was the Messiah. They were communities *of* the Messiah, hence, messianic communities.

[38] "That concerns me about you" is the most literal translation. The word עַל (Strong's G5228) matches the Hebrew, and can mean upon, over, unto, against, toward, or concerning. Context is king. See Matthew 4:6, "He will command His angels *concerning* thee." I can't imagine Love-Incarnate coming *against* His beloved who is suffering for His namesake. Rather, I see compassionate advice, so that the enemy is not able to find a foothold and gain leverage against them.

where you stepped away from it, and do the first works.

'If however you don't, I will come for your sake,[39] and I will cause a shaking[40] of your menorah, if you don't restore yourself. Except you have this to your credit: That you are detesting the works of the Nicolaitans,[41] those things which I myself am also detesting.

'He who has ears, let him hear what the Spirit is speaking to the messianic communities. And to he who is in victory[42] I will give from the tree of life to eat, which exists in the Paradise of God.'"

---

[39] "For your sake" is the same word, עַל (Strong's G5228), "concerning," as above. However a literal translation, "I will come concerning you," misses the meaning. "For your sake" stays true to the root work, but is smoother in English.

[40] It is impossible for the word to imply that Jesus will "remove" the church. The Aramaic root is based on trembling, like an earthquake. So the image is that of something being shaken, stirred, or be moved about.

[41] The seventh-century Western Church Father Isidore of Seville wrote in Etymologies, Book VIII, The Church and Sects, "The Nicolaites (Nicolaita) are so called from Nicolaus, deacon of the church of Jerusalem [Acts 6:5], who, along with Stephen and the others, was ordained by Peter. He abandoned his wife because of her beauty, so that whoever wanted to might enjoy her; the practice turned into debauchery, with partners being exchanged in turn." Stephen A. Barney, W. J. Lewis, J. A. Beach and Oliver Berghof (ed.) The Etymologies of Isidore of Seville, Cambridge University Press, 2006, p. 175.

[42] This is mind-blowing: the root word means clear, guiltless, righteous, deserving, or worthy (see Marcus Jastrow's, pp. 397) in Talmudic and Midrashic literature. But in the Peshitta, it seems to have carried an implication that to be righteous was to be victorious or to have overcome (see J. Payne Smith's pp. 115). In short, the victory is a theological one, afforded vicariously through the death and resurrection of Jesus. We are living *from* victory, *His* victory, which affords us right standing. An amplified translation might read, "to he who is living from Christ's victory." Hence, "in victory" (the Aramaic has a participle, but -ing would be awkward, so I've added "in" at the front of "victory" to reflect the concept that we are constantly in Christ's victory).

2 SECOND LOVE LETTER: SMYRNA

Smyrna could be likened to Miami, Florida. It is situated on the Aegean coast, and enjoys a favorable climate. The region had a large Jewish population, leading to hostility towards those among them who embraced Yeshua as their Messiah. Smyrna was also home to Polycarp, an incredible early church father who was a direct disciple of John the Apostle. He, and several other Believers faced great persecution and death in Smyrna.

REVELATION 2:8–11:

> "And to the messenger who is of the messianic community of Smyrna write: 'Thus says the First and the Last, he who was dead and lives.
>
> 'I know your hardship and your poverty – except you are rich! – and of the blasphemy of those who say to themselves,

"Judaic! Judaic!"[43] when they are not, except they are of the synagogue of Satan.

'Do not fear at any point that which is being schemed for you to experience. Behold! The Devil is scheming[44] to have you thrown into the jail house; he will be testing you, and there will be suffering to you for ten days – be faithful unto death, and I will give to you a crown of life.

'He who has ears, let him hear what the Spirit is speaking to the messianic communities. He who is in victory will not be litigated[45] by a second death."'

---

[43] BFBS has "Jewish," or "Judeans." But the Crawford "Judaic" makes more sense.
[44] The Syriac adds two instances of the same verb, "Schemed" and "Scheming." This is fascinating. The text seeks to make clear that plans of evil come from Satan, not God! See 1 John 1:5 and James 1:17.
[45] The Aramaic נֵהַר (Strong's G2873) has a legal sense, and can mean to dispute, to wrong, or to litigate. While I understand translators taking this to mean a suffered wrong or harm, it is more theologically accurate to maintain the legal tone, since Jesus has manifested Himself as High Priest to those who were once under the curse of the Law, and stand to watch their country suffer litigation from the Law.

3 THIRD LOVE LETTER: PERGAMUM

Pergamum was to its region then what Hollywood is to us today. Celebrities back then weren't movie starts, they were the gods. In Pergamum you would have found temples and shrines dedicated to all the major deities of the day: Zeus, Dionysius, Demeter, Asclepius, Trajan, Isis, Athena, and so on. People flocked from all over the Roman Empire to consult with mediums, ask for healing powers to come over ailing bodies, and participate in rituals. Hence, this was Satan's throne.

REVELATION 2:12–17

"And to the messenger who is in the messianic community of Pergamum write: 'Thus says he who has the sharp sword of two edges of His mouth.[46]

I know where you dwell, a region where Satan has his throne.

[46] "Of his mouth" is found in the Syriac, but not in BFBS.

But you are holding tight in my name, and have not denied my faith, and in the days when you and my faithful witness contended for the sake of all my faithful witnesses, he was murdered among you,[47] and was made a spectacle where Satan dwells.[48]

'Except there is a small thing that concerns me about you, that there are those who are holding tight to the doctrine of Balaam, him who taught Balak to throw a stumbling block before the children of Israel: to eat sacrifices of idols and to commit fornication.[49]

'There are also those of you who are holding tight to the

---

47 "And in the days… among you." This translation is from David Bauscher. He comments, "Greek has 'of Antipas.' 'Antipas' in Aramaic would be opytna, opyjna or oapytna. Frankly this does not look like any Aramaic word in the text, so I don't see the explanation for the Greek reading based on word similarity in Aramaic. I do see that the Aramaic verse speaks of 'My witness' and does not name him. This may have presented a problem to a Greek translator who seems to have also played the role of editor as well. A second phrase – 'for the sake of all My witnesses' is missing in the Greek texts; after careful inspection, I saw that 'for the sake of all' – 'Mettul d'col' was probably translated as the Greek name Antipav – 'Antipas,' which strange to say, means 'For the cause of all,' from two Greek words, anti – 'for, instead of, for the cause of' + pav – 'all, every'. So may the Greek translator have put a name to 'My witness' as 'Antipas.'" The Aramaic English Interlinear Peshitta Bible, pp. 2745.

48 "Was made a spectacle where Satan dwells" is found in BFBS.

49 This fornication equals idolatry formula takes place twice in Revelation (here, and 2:18-29), and is a clearly Hebraic allusion. The Israel story, time after time, depicts the children of Abraham being led into idolatry by way of fornication. Solomon is perhaps the greatest illustration of this. Moreover, citing Jewish sources, Pseudo-Philo's recounting of the Balaam narrative follows this fornication equals idolatry pattern: "And then Balaam said to him 'Come let us plan what you should do to them. Pick out the beautiful women who are among us and in Midian, and station them naked and adorned with gold and precious stones before them. And when they see them and lie with them, they will sin against their LORD and fall into your hands; for otherwise you cannot fight against them'" (Ps-Philo 18:13-14 [Harrington, OTP]).
And the Testament of Reuben suggest that fornication leads to idolatry: "So then, my children, observe all the things that I commanded you, and do not sin, for the sin of promiscuity is the pitfall of life, separating man from God and leading toward idolatry, because it is the deceiver of the mind and the perceptions, and leads youths down to hell before their time" (Test. Reub. 4:6-7 [Kee, OTP]).

doctrine of the Nicolaitans, in like manner.[50]

'Repent therefore, but if not, I will come for your sake, immediately, and I will cause them to have an encounter[51] with the sword of my mouth.

'Now he who has ears, let him hear what the Spirit is speaking to the messianic communities. To he who is in victory, I will give of the manna that is hidden, and I will give him a small white stone, and upon the small stone, a new name,[52] whose inscription no man knows but he who receives it.'"

[50] As the footnote in the letter to the Ephesians indicated, the practices of the Nicolaitans was linked to fornication and spiritual practices ("doctrine").
[51] Most Bible's read, "make war." This is poor theology and a misuse of the text. The word means "to join, to come near, to touch." See Marcus Jastrow's, pp. 1410. The Aphel Imperative denotes causative verb, hence, "cause them to encounter."
[52] This mention of a small stone with a name upon is would have easily reminded the Jewish reader of God's blueprints for Aaron's priestly garments in Exodus 28:6-14: "Take two onyx stones and engrave on them the names of the sons of Israel." But here the stones are no longer black (onyx), but they are white, since they are not longer guilty of sin, but washed clean by the blood of Jesus.

4 FOURTH LOVE LETTER: THYATIRA

You can think of Thyatira as a blue-collar city, much like Detroit. And in the same way blue-collar cities are known to have strong unions, Thyatira had several trade guilds. But these guilds came with spiritual practices associated with them (ie. Freemasons), and the worship of Apollo, the local deity, was customary. Lydia, from Acts 16:14, was from Thyatira, and she was a textile trader.

REVELATION 2:18–29

> "And to the messenger who is in the messianic community which is in Thyatira write, 'Thus says the Son of God, he who has eyes like flames of fire and his feet like the brass of Lebanon.
>
> 'I know your works, and your love, and your faith, and your servanthood, and your perseverance; and your latter works are greater than the first.
>
> 'Except there is a great thing that concerns me about you,

because you condone your wife[53] Jezebel[54] who says concerning herself that she is a prophetess,[55] and she teaches and causes my servants be deceived,[56] to be fornicating[57] and eating the sacrifices of idols.[58]

---

[53] The Byzantine Greek mss. (Majority text) agrees with "your wife".

[54] Who was Jezebel? This passage needs to be understood in light of Rev 3:10, that an hour of testing was to come (at that time) upon the Known World and the Land of Israel. Jezebel was mostly likely a personification of Israel, as John's prophecy was for a Jewish audience and in the spirit and tradition of his prophetic forerunners: See Isaiah 50:1; Ezekiel 16:1-63; Jeremiah 3:1-25; Zechariah 5:5-11; Hosea 1:3 (and also Galatians 4:21–31). John does this again in Revelation 17–19, personifying Israel as a great harlot. **"Jezebel" here may also be a specific reference to the religious leadership within the Holy Land** and their relationship to the rulers (like king Ahab) over Judea and surrounding regions, as they were Roman puppet kings. This led to compromises of the Law (offering Roman sacrifices in the Temple) and a hardness of heart (see John 19:6–15).

[55] Another juxtaposition is presented here: Jezebel in the OT tried to violently silence the voice of the prophets in Israel. Here, presuming Jezebel is apostate Israel, is attempting to silence the prophetic voices of Jesus' followers by imposing her "prophetic" voice and deceptive Law-based doctrine (see Galatians 3).

[56] This is the exact same verb used to describe the deception that Satan was restrained from causing in Revelation chapter 20. Another translation could be, "causes my servants to forget/wander in err."

[57] Fornication here is "less likely a literal charge than a metaphor describing her positive relations with Greco-Roman society" (*The Jewish Annotated New Testament, Second Edition*, ed. Amy-Jill Levine and Marc Zvi Brettler, Accordance electronic ed. (New York: Oxford University Press, 2017), 544). Adultery is often also a metaphor for idolatry. See Jer 3.6–11. This may also hint at systemic hypocrisy. Take for instance the infamous story in the Mishnah of Rabban Gamliel, who visited a bathhouse in Acre (west of Galilee) which featured a nude statue of Aphrodite, the goddess of sexuality. "Idolatry thus is no longer about the actual making and worshipping of idols. It is, rather, a metaphor for what happens whenever a Jew loses his or her focus upon the tenets and ideals of the covenant with God." Avery-Peck, Alan J., "Idolatry in Judaism", in: Encyclopaedia of Judaism. Consulted online on 11 May 2018. <http://dx.doi.org.proxy.lib.umich.edu/10.1163/1872 9029_EJ_COM_0080>

[58] While Jesus walked the earth, the Temple rulers had instituted daily sacrifices to the Roman Emperors, who were considered to be divine. As Josephus recounts, "Petronius then quieted them, and said to them, 'Will you then make war against Caesar?' The Jews said, 'We offer sacrifice twice every day for Caesar, and for the Roman people'" (Wars; 2:10:4). This was most likely a Zevach Sh'lamim, a Peace Offering, since it was political tokenism between Rome and Judea. **Peace Offerings were eaten by the priests and their families**. The seduction then, seems to be a societal easing toward Roman culture and religious practices (Lev 17.10–14). The mix between Judea and Rome is further illustrated in Rev 17 to 20.

'But I gave her time for repentance,[59] and she did not desire to return from her fornication.

'Behold! I will throw her down[60] onto a death bed[61], and those who commit adultery with her into great oppression,[62] except that they repent of their works.[63]

'And her sons I shall execute by a penalty of death[64], and all the messianic communities will know that I search the reins and the hearts, and I will give to every one of you according to your

---

[59] This time of repentance was the forty-year window, from 30 to 70 AD, where the New Covenant and Old Covenant periods overlapped. The end of the Old Covenant period was marked by the destruction of the Temple in Jerusalem, causing animal sacrifices to literally cease from that day forward. I speak of the forty-year transition period at length in my book, Revelation: Dawn of This Age.

[60] Same verb used in Revelation 20:3. But here, Jesus is not "throwing down" in anger. His is the same yesterday, today and forevermore. He is the one who raised the woman caught in adultery (Jn 8:2–11). He is the one who could have extinguished the life of Saul of Tarsus because he killed the first followers of Jesus. Yet Jesus instead came to Saul in love, and loved covered over a multitude of sin. And even though Israel was subject to the consequences of violating the Law of Moses, Romans chapters 9, 10 and 11 reminds us of God's grand love story; "all Israel shall live" (Aramaic text, Rom 11:26).

[61] The Aramaic here is "bier," a mobile cot for the dead (see Luke 7:14). The Greek uses κλίνη (Mt 9:2, Lk 5:18), a cot for the lame and sick. But the context clearly prefers the Aramaic. The word image is that Jezebel is to be carried on a bier to a funeral pyre, a place of burning the dead. This metaphor may also be an illusion to the Gehenna fire of Jeremiah (Jeremiah 7:31–32, 32:35, 19:2–6, 19:11–14), which is echoed by Jesus (Matt 23:33), which became a symbol of Jerusalem being burned to the ground by a foreign power (Babylon, then Rome) as a result of the fires of idolatry lit within the hearts of God's covenant people.

[62] Referring to the Roman invasion of Judea from 67 to 70 AD, resulting in the massacre of (according to Josephus) over 1,000,000 Jews, and the enslavement of tens of thousands. The oppression did not come because Jesus ran out of patience. Rather, it was a prophetic fulfilment based on the words of Moses and the contractual obligations of the Law, outlined in Deuteronomy 28:15–68, 29:22–30:10, 31:14–22, and 32:1–43.

[63] This repentance is explained in Galatians 3:10 and 4:21–31, and was specific to a Jewish audience.

[64] This is a difficult passage to translate. The root word is from the Hebrew, "to cut," in the sense of using a sword on an enemy. But word here אֶקְטֻול has a judicial sense, like a judge finding someone guilty of the death penalty (see William Jennings' Lexicon pp. 102, and Marcus Jastrow's pp. 1349). What is emphatic here is that we do not have Jesus slaughtering someone because they did not repent in time.

works.[65]

'I say to you and to the rest who are in Thyatira, all of those who do not have this doctrine, those who have not "known the depths of Satan," as they say, I won't throw down, concerning you, another burden.

'That which you have, therefore, be holding fast until I come.

'Now to him who is in victory and practices my works, I shall give authority over the peoples,

'to shepherd them with a staff of iron[66], and like the vessels of a potter you will shape[67] them in the same manner I have also received of my Father.[68]

'And I shall give him the Star of the Morning.[69]

'He who has ears, let him hear what the Spirit is speaking to the messianic communities.

---

[65] An alternate translation, from the Crawford Codex may be, "I search the bride and the heart, and I give to you as women bridal veils, according to your works." Because this is based on Greg Glaser's transcription alone, I don't yet have the confidence to make it official. Nevertheless, it fits the theme of Hagar and Sarah, the Bride and the Whore; this theme being prevalent in Jeremiah and Revelation.

[66] Iron means unbreakable authority, whereas wood would be subject to fractures.

[67] The primary definition of this word is to "grind," as one who sharpens a blade or one who crushes wheat in a mill. Given the context of pottery (the word can also mean clay), the implication is the same, to grind or shape in order to make something better and more useful (a sharp blade or flour for bread).

[68] Verses 26 and 27 speak of the Great Commission to disciple nations. And we do this in the manner of Ephesians 4:11–15, the five-fold ministry, "for the equipping of the saints for the work of ministry, for the building up of the body of Christ; until we all attain to the unity of the faith, and of the knowledge of the Son of God, to a mature man, to the measure of the stature which belongs to the fullness of Christ." We shepherd like the Good Shepherd: "As the Father has sent me, so I send you" (John 20:21).

[69] Jesus is the Morning Star (Num 24:17; 2 Pet 1:19; Rev 22;15), and he gives himself to us! "Therefore be imitators of God, as beloved children; and walk in love, just as Christ also loved you and **gave Himself up for us**" (Eph 5:1–2). Historically, messianic imagery was often affiliated with celestial object. For instance, the second-century Jewish messianic figure Simeon Bar Kochba ("son of the star").

5 FIFTH LOVE LETTER: SARDIS

This region was well known for its abundance of gold, much like the Sierra Nevada during the California gold rush. Like all the other regions in the seven love letters, Sardis also had a very large Jewish community, and even a prominent synagogue.[70] Sardis was founded by the Lydian king Gyges, who in Hebrew translates as Gog (of Magog). Interestingly, the Persian King Cyrus II (aka Cyrus the Great) later sacked the city through a hidden entrance, coming unexpectedly, like a "thief in the night."

REVELATION 3:1–6

> And to the messenger who is in the messianic community of Sardis write, 'Thus says he who has to Himself sevenfold Spirit[71] of God and seven stars. I know your works and the

[70] Josephus, Ant 14.235,259–61.

[71] Also found in Rev 1:4, "sevenfold Spirit" can be translated literally as "seven Spirits." Again, this is thoroughly Jewish language. See 1 Enoch 20.1–8; or the liturgical text from Qumran Cave 4, 4QShirShabb (Songs of the Sabbath Sacrifice).

name that you have, and those of you who are alive, and those of you who are dead.

'Now wake up and prop up the remainder of those who are ready to die, [72] for I have not found your works to be made complete before God.[73]

'Cause yourself to remember what you heard and received; take heed and return.[74] But if you do not wake up, I will come for your sake as a thief, and you will not know what hour I will come for your sake.[75]

'But I have a few names in Sardis, those who have not stained their priestly garments, and they walk before me in white and they are worthy.

'He who overcomes thusly is clothed with a white priestly garment[76], and I shall not erase his name from the Book of

[72] "The one who has found his life will lose it, and the one who has lost his life on My account will find it." Matthew 10:39 (also 16:25). Those who are dead in verse 1 are those who have not been born again. They are still dead in their sins. Those ready to die are those ready to be born again, they put to death the flesh in order to come alive (Rom 8:13). John uniquely develops the notion of a First Death, Second Death, and First Resurrection, Second Resurrection in both his Gospel and Revelation. I discuss this at length in Revelation: Dawn of All Hope.
[73] This is what Paul called "dead works" (Heb 6:1; 9:14; Philippians 3:4-9), which is to live an outward life of piety without the inward regeneration of the Spirit (Eph.2:8-10; Heb.11:6). See also John 3:35–36.
[74] "what you heard and received." This is almost a direct quote from First John 1:1–3. In other words, "remember all the things John taught you about Me (Jesus)!"
[75] There is a layered implication here: to the immediate audience, Jesus will come much like Cyrus, and will bring a refiner's fire and launder's soap to his people in Sardis, calling them higher and maturing them into His image (Mal 3:2; Rom 8:29). In broader context, Jesus was coming to oversee the fulfilment of his prophetic words in Matthew 23 and 24 (and Luke 19:28–44; 21:5–24): the fulfillment of Deuteronomy 28:15–68, 29:22–30:10, 31:14–22, and 32:1–43. And the Roman invasion in 67 AD was unexpected, like a thief in the night.
[76] Here and in 3:4 above, the word "priestly" in not in the text, but it is implied, so I have added it ("priestly garment"). When the Sanhedrin, a tribunal in Judea, judged a priest to be fit for service, he was clothed in white. See Samuel Burder, Oriental Customs, Michigan: University of Michigan, 1923, pp. 387. Thus, when we are born anew in Jesus, we become a royal priesthood (Isaiah 61:6; Exodus 19:6; 1 Peter 2:9; Revelation 1:6).

Life,[77] and I shall confess his name before my Father and before his angels.[78]

'He who has ears, let him hear what the Spirit is speaking to the messianic communities.

[77] The notion of a "Book of Life" is not unique to John. It is in fact a key symbol of Jewish identity, taking us all the way back to Exodus: "But now, if You will forgive their sin, very well; but if not, please wipe me [Moses] out from Your book which You have written!" However, the Lord said to Moses, "Whoever has sinned against Me, I will wipe him out of My book. But go now, lead the people where I told you. Behold, My angel shall go before you; nevertheless on the day when I punish, I will punish them for their sin" (Ex 32:32–34). The context of Exodus 32 is the sin of the Golden Calf, and Moses trying to make atonement for their sin (32:30). He was unable, because only Jesus would be able to make atonement for the sin of Israel (read all of Hebrews!).

[78] A reminder of the words of Jesus in Matt 10:32 and Luke 12:8.

6 SIXTH LOVE LETTER: PHILADELPHIA

Philadelphia to me is much like the Philadelphia of the 1970s portrayed in the first *Rocky* movie; a blue-collar region with down-an-out people struggling to recover economically. They suffered physical and financial devastation caused by a series of earthquakes.[79] The city was also renamed twice: first, to Neocaesarea (New Caesar), and perhaps just months or short years after John wrote these words, to Flavius. The second name was after the new Roman emperor Vespasian, the 'Nebuchadnezzar' who has started the campaign against Israel that his son Titus would finish. This "new name" reference will come up again shortly in the text below. Lastly, the "synagogue of Satan"[80] here gives us a clue to the strong adversity Jewish followers of Jesus would have faced from their fellow kinsmen in the region.

---

[79] Pliny, Nat. 2.86.200; Strabo, Geogr. 12.8.18; 13.4.10.

[80] In no way does this reference to a "synagogue of Satan" suggest that John became anti-Semitic. John was a Jew through and through. It simply suggests that Jesus was exposing the hearts of a certain group of people in a specific region. For instance, Satan was able to penetrate the heart of Judas because of his hardness of heart, causing Him to betray Jesus (Jn 13:27). Hardness of heart therefore could have led this group of people to fall under the same deception that blinded Saul of Tarsus, leading him to persecute the Saints.

REVELATION 3:7-13

And to the messenger of the messianic community of Philadelphia write: 'Thus says the Holy Truth, he who has the key of David, who opens and there is none who shuts, and he shuts and there is none who opens.[81]

'I know your works, and behold! I have given an open door before you which no man can shut, because you have little power, and you have practiced my word and have not denied my name.[82]

'And behold! I have given from the synagogue of Satan, those who say concerning themselves that they are Jews and are not, but they are lying, behold! I will make them come and prostrate themselves before your feet,[83] and they will know that I burn with love for you.[84]

'For the sake of you who keep the word of my perseverance, I will also keep you from the trial that is foreordained to come upon all of the Known World[85], to test the inhabitants of The

---

[81] Quoted from David Bauscher, who comments: "The Crawford text of this verse conforms more closely to The Peshitta reading of Isaiah 22:22 than does the Greek or The Harklean Aramaic text, and also to the Hebrew present participles, "who shuts", "who opens", more closely than the Greek does. Even the Aramaic phrases & there is none who closes & there is none who opens are identical in The Peshitta of Isaiah where the black highlighted letters are shown in bold type, while the Harklean has 'no man shuts' and 'no man opens,' conforming to the Greek readings." The Aramaic English Interlinear Peshitta Bible, pp. 2745.

[82] It is my belief that Jesus was taking something these Jews had experienced personally; the doors of the synagogue they once attended being shut in their face and their re-entry barred because they could not deny that Yeshua was the Messiah, and uses what the enemy meant for evil to catapult them into destiny.

[83] We have no known historical account of what this looked like. But we do know that God opposes the proud and gives grace to the humble.

[84] This word in Aramaic אַחֲבַת literally means to burn, or to be lit, with passionate love. How beautiful is the love of Jesus towards you and I!

[85] This is the first time in this book that we have come across a reference to a geographical region beyond Israel. Up to now, we have seen "The Land" הָאָרֶץ which typically refers to the Land of Israel. But now we have תֵּבֵל (H8398), the whole inhabitable world, or, the known world. Historically, this would have been

Land.[86]

'I come immediately. Hold fast whatever you have, that no man take your crown.[87]

'And he who is in victory I will make them a pillar in the Temple of God,[88] and to the outside world he will not go to again[89], and I shall write upon him the Name of my God, and the name of the city – the New Jerusalem – which descends from my God,[90]

---

synonymous with the Roman Empire, given its vast expanse. For instance, Matt 24:14, "This gospel of the kingdom shall be preached ***in the whole world*** as a testimony to all the nations, and then the end will come." Or, Col 1:5–6, "the gospel which has come to you, just as ***in all the world*** also it is bearing fruit." Revelation 3:11 picks up on the fulfillment of Matt 24, as Paul confirms in Col 1.

[86] In contrast to the inhabited world, the Roman Empire, we shift back to The Land of Israel, since these prophecies are for them almost exclusively. An amplified translation might read, "I also shall keep you from the trial that is foreordained to come upon all of the Roman Empire, to test the Jewish inhabitants of the Land of Israel."

[87] The destruction of Israel (Judea at the time), known as the Jewish-Roman War, did not only affect the Jews within the Holy Land, but also abroad. Jews in places like Philadelphia would soon be targets of Roman hate as well: "The raising of the standard of revolt against Rome, however, had its repercussions throughout the whole of Palestine and a large part of the Diaspora… The news of the revolt, and especially of the slaughter of the Roman garrison at Jerusalem, had a disastrous consequence for the Jewish population… This bloody act naturally provoked Jewish reprisals. The Gentile cities of **Philadelphia**… were attacked, the neighbouring Syrian villages were laid waste, and without doubt Gentiles throughout Palestine generally perished as victims of Jewish fanaticism." S. G. F. Brandon, M.A., D.D., The Fall of Jerusalem and the Christian Church, A Study of the Effects of the Jewish Overthrow of A.D. 70 on Christianity (London: S.P.C.K, 1951) at 158.

[88] Flowing in line with the Roman invasion of Israel (also prophesied by Jesus in Luke 19:28–44 and 21:5–24), which resulted in the beloved Temple being destroyed, Jesus reminds them of a New Temple, his Bride (1 Cor 3:16–17; Eph 2:19–22; 1 Pet 2:5).

[89] Jesus speaks to both the Diaspora and those forced to leave Judea (either because of the current persecution, or the imminent Roman invasion), as a future hope that when He restores all things (Acts 1:6), they will no longer be displaced.

[90] See Revelation 21. It is important to note that Revelation ends with heaven coming down to this physical earth, and this earth becomes Eden once more!

and my new Name.[91]

'Now he who has ears, let him hear what the Spirit is speaking to the messianic communities."

[91] In the same way the Yahweh God renamed several Old Testament figures, and Jesus likewise with some of His disciples, we too, are given new names – that is to say, a new purpose and destiny as sons and daughters made in His image.

7 SEVENTH LOVE LETTER: LAODICEANS

This region was like Manhattan; high rollers and bankers. A major center of commerce and trade, it had at one point five agoras (shopping malls), and a 20,000 person auditorium. They were so wealthy that when an earthquake in 66 AD devastated the city of Laodicea, they refused the Roman relief fund and used their own cash to rebuild the ruined city. Further to this point, you may have noticed that I called this letter, "Laodiceans," not, "Laodicea." This was intentional, and the explanation is in the footnote below.

It should not be a surprise to us to learn that Laodicea had a strong Jewish community.[92] The region was also known to be a medical hub, specifically for collyrium (eye-salve). Lastly, natural mineral water sources flowed in to Laodicea from Hierapolis (and still does today. Check it out online, it is stunning!), and water from Colossae; one source hot, the other cold. These water sources served as a powerful illustration in Jesus' admonition below.

[92] Josephus, Ant. 12.147–53.

REVELATION 3:14–22

"And to the messenger of the messianic community of the Laodiceans[93] write, 'Thus says the Amen, the Faithful and True Witness, and the Genesis[94] of the Creation of God.

'I know your works; you are not cold and you are not hot. It would be best if you were either cold or were hot,[95]

'but you are lukewarm and neither cold nor hot.[96] I am

[93] The Aramaic reads Laodiceans, not, Laodicea, referring to the people, not the place. Why? Because Laodicea, Colossae and Hierapolis were destroyed by an earthquake in AD 66. Meaning there was no city to write to at the time, just the people who once lived in it, until it was rebuilt (see Thayer's Greek-English Lexicon under the entry for "Laodicea", and Bishop Lightfoot, Colossians and Philemon, pp. 274–300). This supports a date as early as 66 AD for the writing of Revelation.

[94] The Aramaic and Hebrew are the same word, רֵאשִׁית (H7225) "the beginning." But the word goes much deeper than that. The Book of Genesis in the Torah is called בְּרֵאשִׁית "In The Beginning," named after the first words in the first sentence of the book (this is the case for all five books of the Pentateuch). Jesus was the author of creation, and therefore, He *is* the Genesis (John 1:3, 10; Col 1:16; Rom 11:36; Heb 1:2).

[95] By referring to the uniqueness of each source of water, Jesus ultimately leads his listeners to understanding that they cannot mix covenants (old wine vs new). The waters from Hierapolis and Colossae were completely different from one another, and each served a purpose. But mixed together, the waters were useless for healing properties (hot mineral water) or for drinking (cold spring water). This mixing here is similar to the teaching found in Matthew 9:17 and Luke 5:35–39, and is powerfully illustrated by Jesus at the wedding in Cana (John 2:10).

[96] They were neither mindful of piety through their upbringing under the Law, nor were they pursuing a deepening in their relationship with Jesus. Rather, they were caught up in the Manhattan lifestyle of "money makes the world go 'round," and lost sight of their identity in Yahweh God through Yeshua.

preparing to be causing you to be restored[97] by my mouth,[98]

'because you said[99] that you are wealthy, and, "I have become powerful, and on account of nothing do I lack,"[100] but you are not knowing that you are weak, and miserable, and blind,[101] and naked.

'My royal counsel to you:[102] Be buying from me gold proved by fire, that you may become wealthy, and be clothing yourself with white priestly garments, that you not unveil the shame of your nakedness, and be blinded by eye-salve, that you may see.

'I have compassion for those who I admonish and instruct. Be

---

[97] The Aramaic, מַתְבֻוֹתְ, is in the Aphel (like the Hebrew Hiphil) Infinitive Construct, a causative action. The word itself means "to return," "to change direction," "to restore," "to answer," or, "to vomit." However, "vomit" has very few lexical examples, while the other translation options have several. Second, the same root word is used again in 3:19, but is translated as repent. So how can one be repent, and the other to vomit? And theologically, it doesn't fit the character of Jesus at all. See verse 19, "whom he has *compassion* for."

[98] Man does not live by bread (or material things), but by the word of life that proceed from the mouth of Jesus (Mat 4:4; Jn 6:68). His Word would wash them like the mineral waters that flowed into the region (Eph 5:26).

[99] Because calamity came by their mouth, Jesus will restore by his mouth.

[100] Laodicea, a center for banking (think Manhattan), was well known for its affluence. Now, it was common for the Roman Empire to provide a relief fund for cities hit with natural disasters, such as earthquakes. But the Laodiceans were so wealthy that Tacitus, the Roman historian, writing of the effects of the 66 AD earthquake on Laodicea, remarked, "without any relief from us, [Laodicea] recovered itself from its own resources." Tacitus, Annals, 14:27.

[101] The Aramaic does not have both, "and poor, and blind," like the Greek, but just one. Most Aramaic translations opt for "poor" over "bind." But I have chosen "blind" for two reasons. First, as Bauscher notes, "The DSS Aramaic Simkat & Mim (each word has both letters in corresponding places) appear more similar to each other than the Estrangela counterparts s & m, thus making it more likely a translator would confuse the DSS script words than the Estrangela script words. The DSS letters -Yodh & Nun are also much more similar (-Yodh & Kap - also) than in the other scripts" (The Aramaic English Interlinear Peshitta Bible, pp. 2746). So there is a likelihood of scribal error. Second, there are several synonyms for poverty in verse 17, so "poor" is unnecessary. Especially when Jesus provides the solution to all that hinders them, including sight. Also note that nakedness was a sign of extreme poverty.

[102] The word, מַלֵךְ, is based on the root, "king," or the root verb, "to reign." Thus, the variant, "to counsel," carries with it a monarchal tone, as the advice is coming from the King of Kings.

aroused to zeal therefore and return.'[103]

'Behold! I stand at the door and I am knocking. If a man listens to my voice and will open the door, then I will enter and I will dine with him, and he with me.[104]

'And he who is in victory I will grant him to be sitting with me upon my throne, just as I have overcome and I sit with my Father on his throne.

'Now he who has ears, let him hear what the Spirit is speaking to the messianic communities."

[103] This is a summons to a first-love encounter with Jesus, much like we read in the letter to the Ephesians. The abiding love that Jesus speaks of at length in John 15 and 17 is the key to maintaining this fires of this love stoked and ablaze.

[104] How beautiful is this picture of an invitation to intimate covenant union with Jesus! In the same way he broke the bread and sipped the wine of covenant with His disciples, we are invited to sit at that same table with Him in matrimonial intimacy (See also Exodus 24:1–18).

EPILOGUE: THE TRIUMPH OF THE CROSS: CHAPTERS 4 – 5

Perhaps one of the most beautiful moments I have had with Jesus while studying His Scriptures was back in 2018 when I was reading Revelation 4 and 5. My mind was caught up in imagining what it looked like, what it felt like, to see what John saw. Suddenly, the scene in my mind changed without notice, and I was watching John and Mary at the foot of the cross, beholding Jesus' in his final moments before offering up his life.

"Now beside the cross of Jesus stood His mother… So when Jesus saw His mother, and the disciple whom He loved standing nearby, He said to His mother, "Madam, behold, your son!" Then He said to the disciple, "Behold, your mother!" And from that hour the disciple took her into his own household." John 19:25–27 (NASB)

It was at that moment that I realized something: because John, the beloved friend of Jesus, endured until the end and witnesses the triumph of the cross from earth's perspective – which looked as if Jesus was defeated, humiliated, and killed from man's eyes, years later John was invited to **see the exact same event**, the triumph of the cross, from heaven's perspective!

When John was invited to "come up here" (Rev 4:1), it was to have a view from above; a direct contrast to the view John had of the cross from below. While a few dozen men mocked from earth's perspective, millions upon millions of angels worshipped in heaven. While he was crucified like a criminal here, he was ushered in as a king there!

By now I was in tears, because I could see what John had first seen when Jesus was on the cross. Yet we know that for the joy set before Him endured the cross – you and I were that joy!

> *"Jesus, the originator and perfecter of the faith, who for the joy set before Him endured the cross, despising the shame, and has sat down at the right hand of the throne of God." Hebrews 12:2*

Therefore, I invite you now to not only read but envision the enthronement that followed the enfleshment of our Lord and Saviour, Jesus Christ, Yeshua Messiah. He is indeed the King of all Kings, Lord of all Lords, President of all Presidents, Prime Minister of all Prime Ministers! He is the God of all hope (Rom 15:13), so get your hopes sky high!

> *"For a Child will be born to us, a Son will be given to us;*
> *And the government will rest on His shoulders;*
> *And His name will be called Wonderful Counselor, Mighty God,*
> *Eternal Father, Prince of Peace.*
> *There will be no end to the increase of His government or of peace*
> *On the throne of David and over his kingdom,*
> *To establish it and to uphold it with justice and righteousness*
> *From then on and forevermore.*
> *The zeal of the Lord of armies will accomplish this."*
> *Isaiah 9:6–7 (NASB)*

Let us now behold the triumph of the cross from heaven's perspective.

REVELATION 5

"And one of the elders said to me, "Stop weeping; behold, the Lion that is from the tribe of Judah, the Root of David, has overcome so as to be able to open the scroll and its seven seals."

And I saw between the throne (with the four living creatures) and the elders a Lamb standing, as if slaughtered, having seven horns and seven eyes, which are the seven spirits of God sent out into all the earth. And He came and took the scroll out of the right hand of Him who sat on the throne…
Then I looked, and I heard the voices of many angels around the throne and the living creatures and the elders; and the number of them was myriads of myriads, and thousands of thousands, saying with a loud voice,

"Worthy is the Lamb that was slaughtered to receive power, wealth, wisdom, might, honor, glory, and blessing."

And I heard every created thing which is in heaven, or on the earth, or under the earth, or on the sea, and all the things in them, saying,

"To Him who sits on the throne and to the Lamb be the blessing, the honor, the glory, and the dominion forever and ever."

And the four living creatures were saying, "Amen." And the elders fell down and worshiped." Revelation 5:5–7, 11–14 (NASB)

How beautiful was that? Especially when compared to the suffering of the cross. Remarkably, Jesus isn't done yet! He didn't ascend and retire. He is still at work:

"For as in Adam all die, so also in Christ all will be made alive. But each in his own order: Christ the first fruits, after that those who are Christ's at His coming, then comes the end, when He hands over the kingdom to our God and Father, when He has abolished all rule and all authority and power. For He must reign until He has put all His enemies under His feet. The last enemy that will be abolished is death." 1 Cor 15:22–26 (NASB)

The Aramaic reads that Jesus must be *continually reigning* until He has put all His enemies under His feet. He is not only on the throne, he is actively ruling from it, and every enemy of God is being crushed by Him, one by one. Because of this, we can co-labour with Christ, yoked to Him in meekness and humility (Mat 11:28–30), and disciple the nations as he commissioned us to do (Mat 28:18; Rev 2:26–27).

Thank you for reading this short work. Blessings over you and your loved ones. Jesus paid a high price for you. Revelation 13:8 reads that Jesus was slain before the foundations of the world. This means that before creation ever took place, He looked ahead and saw you. It means that He counted the cost, and concluded you were worth dying for. You aren't plan B for God. You are His beloved.

Finally, I ask that we live in unity. Let us fulfill the words of Jesus together:

> *"The glory which You have given Me I also have given to them, so that they may be one, just as We are one; I in them and You in Me, that they may be perfected in unity, so that the world may know that You sent Me, and You loved them, just as You loved Me. Father, I desire that they also, whom You have given Me, be with Me where I am, so that they may see My glory which You have given Me, for You loved Me before the foundation of the world." John 17:22–24 (NASB)*

If there is anything you read in this book that you don't agree with, I ask that you lift me up in prayer, that I might grow in the knowledge of God. I ask that you bless, and not curse, so that we do not partner with the wrong spirit. I bless you on your journey of knowing Him more and more. To Him be the glory forever, Amen!

ABOUT THE AUTHOR

Leo De Siqueira has a passion to dig deeper into the Scriptures in order to better understand the heart of God towards mankind. While attending Tyndale University College in Toronto, Leo focused his studies on translating Biblical Hebrew and early church history. He and his wife Melanie have three beautiful children and serve their local church in Calgary, Canada.

www.ingramcontent.com/pod-product-compliance
Lightning Source LLC
LaVergne TN
LVHW011051110826
845149LV00015B/3446

* 9 7 8 1 9 9 9 5 0 6 0 4 9 *